CLOTHING, COSTUMES, and UNIFORMS Throughout AMERICAN HISTORY™

What People Wore During the Westward Expansion

∞ Allison Stark Draper ∞

The Rosen Publishing Group's
PowerKids Press™
New York

For my mother

Published in 2001 by The Rosen Publishing Group, Inc.
29 East 21st Street, New York, NY 10010

First Edition

Book Design: Emily Muschinske

Photo Credits: contents page (Native American blanket) © Lowe Art Museum/SuperStock; pp. 4, 11 © Mercury Archives/Image Bank; pp. 5, 10, 13, 19 © SuperStock; p. 6 © Frederic Remington/SuperStock; p. 7 © Stock Montage/SuperStock; pp. 8, 11 (fur) © Lowell Georgia/CORBIS; pp. 9, 14, 18, 21 © CORBIS; p. 12 © The Huntington Library, Art Collections and Botanical Gardens, San Marino, California/SuperStock; p. 15 © George Catlin/National Gallery of Art/SuperStock; pp. 16, 22 © Frederic Remington/North Wind Pictures; p. 20 © Todd Gipstein/CORBIS.

Draper, Allison Stark.
    What people wore during the westward expansion / Allison Stark Draper.
      p. cm.— (Clothing, costumes, and uniforms throughout American history)
    Summary: This book describes what people wore in the days of westward expansion, discussing the styles of the pioneer men and women, the trappers, and the cowboys.
    ISBN 0-8239-5667-9
    1. Costume—United States—History—Juvenile literature. 2. Costume—West (U.S.)—History—Juvenile literature. 3. United States—Social life and customs—Juvenile literature. 4. United States—History—Colonial period, ca. 1600-1775—Juvenile literature. [1. Costume—West (U.S.)—History. 2. United States—Social life and customs—Colonial period, ca. 1600-1775.] I. Title. II. Series.

GT607 .D69 2000
391'.00978—dc21   00-039162

Contents

Moving West

By the mid-1800s, many people lived on the east coast of the United States. A lot of these people had come to America from other countries. They had come looking for a better life. Cities in the East got so crowded that people began moving west to settle new land. Most people traveled west in covered wagons. The trip was long and difficult. These **pioneers** had to drive through rain, snow, and dust. The pioneers wore sturdy fabrics like wool and corduroy. Men wore high boots to protect themselves from rattlesnakes and prickly pear cacti. Some women traveling west wore bloomer pants under their skirts. Bloomer pants were long pants made out of cotton.

Pioneers traveled west in covered wagons. The journey was long and hard, so they had to wear tough fabrics.

Frontier Men

People in **frontier** towns wore clothes that reminded them of their homes back in the East. They also wore clothes that were tough enough for the West. Men in the West needed clothes that were comfortable when they rode horses and did hard physical work. A man in the West might wear a linen shirt and a **frock coat**. A Western man would also wear a felt hat, riding boots, and spurs. A man in the East would not wear boots or spurs

It was hard work to build towns in the West. That is why men and women had to wear comfortable clothes that lasted a long time.

This frontiersman is wearing sturdy pants, a lightweight shirt, and boots.

because he did not need to ride a horse every day. Western men wore pants made out of jeaning, or denim. They might also wear wool pants and flannel shirts. In the summer, many Western men wore soft **moccasins** instead of boots.

Frontier Women

Clothes for Western women had to be practical. Dresses came down to their ankles. The dresses were made of wool, cotton, or **calico**. Women in the West did not usually wear **corsets**. Corsets were tight and kept a woman from moving freely. Women usually did not wear a lot of **petticoats** under their dresses either. Most women wore cotton **sunbonnets**. Sunbonnets tied over women's hair in the

This women is wearing a calico dress and a sunbonnet. Sunbonnets protected a woman's skin from burning as she worked outside.

8

back and shadowed their faces in the front. This protected their skin from burning.

For dances and parties, women in the West copied what women wore in the East. Frontier women used the same shirt and skirt shapes as Eastern women. They just used less fancy fabric.

Women had to wear comfortable clothes so they could do things like work on their land and ride horses.

Trappers and Lumberjacks

The first Americans in the West were **trappers** and traders. These men often lived in the same area as Native Americans. The trappers copied the Native Americans' clothes. They wore **buckskin** coats with long fringes. The fringes drained off rain. Sometimes the trappers tore the fringes off and used them as string to knot together broken pieces of rope or **harness**.

There were forests north of the Western plains. French and American **lumberjacks** lived in these forests. Lumberjacks wore fur to stay warm. They used sashes made by the

 Lumberjacks wore jeans, flannel shirts, and suspenders. Suspenders are straps worn over a man's shoulders to help hold up his pants.

This person is scraping fur off an animal skin using a sharp tool. The fur will be used to make a piece of clothing.

This woman is preparing animal fur to sell. She is wearing loose-fitting clothes that fit in with her hard lifestyle.

Native Americans to hold up their pants. Lumberjacks either cut their pants short or rolled them up. This kept the pants from getting caught on fallen trees.

Searching for Gold

In 1848, gold was discovered at a **millrace** in California. After this, thousands of people came to the state to search for gold. **Miners** dug in the earth for gold. They blasted **ore** from tunnels or searched for gold nuggets in streams. Miners in the West worked hard, but rarely found gold. They did not have much money for clothes. Miners usually had just one pair of pants. Their pants had patches and were worn out at the knees.

Most miners did not have enough money to buy new clothes. They had to mend the clothes they already owned.

They wore long-sleeved shirts that buttoned to the neck. Over their shirts they wore a vest and sometimes a long jacket. To protect themselves from the sun, miners wore hats with wide brims. Sometimes they copied the Mexican style and wore **sombreros**. If a miner found gold, he liked to show off his wealth. He might wear a ruffled shirt or a brightly colored silk scarf.

Miners who searched for gold in streams often wore out the knees of their pants. Instead of buying new pants, they sewed patches over the knees of their old pants. This miner is wearing a hat with a wide brim to protect his face from the sun.

Clothes of the Plains Indians

A Plains Indian man needed strong, comfortable clothes to fit his **rugged** lifestyle. In the summer, Plains Indian men wore **breechcloths** and soft moccasins. In colder weather, they wore leather shirts and leather coverings for the legs. These were called leggings. Plains women wore longer shirts. Some tribes wore deer or antelope skins. Most tribes scraped the fur or hair off the animal skins. Some northern Native Americans kept the fur or hair on for warmth. During the winter, both men and women wore fur robes. Sometimes men's robes were painted with scenes that showed the brave things they had done.

On the left is a Plains Indian boy dressed in jeans, a beaded vest, and moccasins. This Native American chief on the right is wearing a long leather shirt, leggings, and moccasins. The animal skin held by the woman shows the brave acts of a Plains Indian man.

Cowboys on the Cattle Ranches

Cowboys were Westerners who worked on cattle ranches. Cowboys took care of the cattle. They also made sure the cattle got from one place to another safely. Cowboys spent most of their time on horseback. They wore leather vests to protect themselves from the wind. Almost all cowboys wore leather chaps. Chaps were first worn in Mexico. They looked like Native American leggings. Chaps protected the cowboys' legs from rubbing against the saddle. Early cowboys wore chaps made of stiff cowhide. These chaps were tight and closed down the sides like pants. Later, chaps were looser. They were open on the sides. Sometimes chaps were decorated with buckskin fringes.

Chaps and sombreros were first worn by Mexicans like the man on the left. Americans in the West copied the Mexican way of dressing. The cowboy on the right is wearing chaps, a leather vest, and a hat called a Stetson.

16

Cowboy Clothes

Cowboys wore brightly colored handkerchiefs called bandannas that tied around their necks. Bandannas soaked up sweat. Cowboys also pulled the bandannas up over their noses to keep from breathing dust on the trail. Cowboys wore buckskin gloves. The gloves protected their hands from rope burns and kept them warm. They wore wide-brimmed hats, such as Mexican

This is a picture of movie cowboy Tom Mix. The West made a big difference in how the country saw itself. Mix is wearing a bandanna, chaps, a holster, and a Stetson hat.

18

sombreros. These hats kept the sun and rain off the cowboys' faces. Cowboys also wore pistol belts and **holsters**. They carried pistols to protect themselves from horse and cattle thieves. Sometimes they carried long whips called blacksnake whips to move horses and cattle along. These whips got their name because they looked like long, black snakes.

These men are dressed to suit their lifestyle. Both men are wearing holsters, bandannas, and Stetsons. The man on the left has on fur chaps and leather wristbands.

Spurs and Stetsons

Cowboys wore leather boots with pointed toes. The boots were usually black. They wore steel spurs shaped like spiky wheels on their boots. The spurs were used to urge their horses along. In 1870, a man named John Stetson made a wide-brimmed hat that he named after himself. The Stetson protected the cowboy against sun and rain. He could use it as a pillow or as a bowl. He could also use it to carry water back from a stream. The Stetson was nicknamed the "Boss of the Plains." The Texas Stetson had a four-inch (10.2-cm) brim. It was seven inches (17.8 cm) high. Some Stetsons had hatbands of leather or snakeskin. By 1900, almost every cowboy in America wore a Stetson.

Cowboys used spurs to move their horses along.

The Stetson was so popular that by 1900 almost every cowboy wore one. This is a Stetson hat factory. The machines shown put dents in the top of the Stetson so a cowboy could easily grab the hat with his hand.

The Law Out West

Most Western towns were too small to have police stations. Instead, they had sheriffs. Sheriffs chased **outlaws** and stopped gunfights. Sheriffs did not wear a formal uniform. Their "uniform" was the outfit that many Western men wore. Sheriffs wore white shirts, leather vests, boots with spurs, and Stetsons. A sheriff wore a **badge** to show that he was the sheriff. A sheriff's badge was a solid brass star. It had six points with rounded ends. In the back, the badge had a long pin that was used to attach it to the sheriff's clothes. Like other men and women of the West, sheriffs worked hard. Their clothes had to be as tough as they were.

This sheriff is wearing chaps, a hat with a wide brim, a holster, and sturdy boots. A sheriff's badge was stamped with the name of the area that he protected.

Glossary

badge (BADJ) Something worn to show that a person belongs to a certain job or club.

breechcloths (BREECH-kloths) Cloths worn around the hips.

buckskin (BUK-skin) A strong, soft leather made from the skins of deer.

calico (KA-lih-koh) Cotton fabric printed with small designs.

corsets (KOR-sets) Undergarments worn around the middle of the body that are tightened with laces.

frock coat (FROK KOHT) A man's coat with narrow shoulders and buttons down the front.

frontier (frun-TEER) The edge of settled land.

harness (HAR-nes) The leather straps, bands, and other pieces used to hitch a horse or other animal to a carriage, wagon, or plow.

holsters (HOHL-sters) Leather holders for guns.

lumberjacks (LUM-ber-jaks) People whose job is cutting down trees to make logs.

millrace (MIL-rays) A waterway in which water flows to and from a mill wheel.

miners (MY-nerz) People who work in mines.

moccasins (MOK-kah-sins) Leather shoes originally worn by Native Americans.

ore (OR) A mineral or rock that has enough metal in it to make digging for it worthwhile.

outlaws (OWT-lawz) People who have broken the law and are on the run from the police.

petticoats (PEH-tee-kohts) Underskirts that are usually a little shorter than a woman's outer clothing.

pioneers (PY-uh-neers) One of the first people to settle in a new area.

rugged (RUG-id) Sturdy.

sombreros (som-BRER-ohz) Wide-brimmed hats originally worn by Mexicans.

sunbonnets (SUN BON-its) Cotton bonnets that protected a woman's face from the sun.

trappers (TRAP-erz) People who captured animals and sold their furs.

Index

Web Sites

To find out more about what people wore during the Westward Expansion check out these Web sites:
http://www.americanwest.com/pages/wexpansi.htm
http://www.nps.gov/fola/indians.htm